THINK LIKE A
REALTOR®

A little book about buying and selling
residential real estate through
the eyes of a REALTOR®.

JASON GELIOS

Published by Jason Gelios, IngramSpark and CreateSpace

ISBN 978-0-578-44886-2

All situations shared in this book have been kept confidential and share no knowledge of actual names and places.

Proudly printed in the USA

Cover and interior design by Jason Gelios

Proofread and edited by Patricia Gordon

For business inquiries or multiple copy deals, please visit:
www.JasonGelios.com

For real estate inquiries, please visit:
www.ItsAllAboutTheRealEstate.com

This book is dedicated to my wife, Erica Gelios. For over twenty years she has inspired me to do great things and to always strive for what I want out of life. An unbelievable partner and friend, amazing wife and a fantastic mother. Thanks, E. I Love You.

THE MAIN REASON BEHIND THIS BOOK

One of the main reasons for this book is to dispel a lot of the myths that all real estate agents are the same. The myth that all agents only put a house on the MLS and a sign in the yard. I want to share with you some valuable information and actual situations that have arose where my skills as a REALTOR® were put to a test. This book covers many situations where I have encountered certain real estate topics that you may find helpful. Any personal information, such as names, has been left out due to confidentiality. Nonetheless, these are real situations and real advice.

Real estate can be one of the most emotional experiences most people will go through. When you consider that a home is one of the largest purchases the average person will make, what seems like one small issue can take an emotional toll on a buyer. For example, something as small as a minor leak in the basement of a home could scare someone away even if it might be something that is repairable. In this book I will also share why it is important to have a REALTOR® on your side.

One of the main reasons why it is important to have a REALTOR® is because we are professionals in dealing with such issues as they arise or sometimes BEFORE they arise if possible. We have been through it all and have experience with multiple issues firsthand. A REALTOR® knows how to navigate through issues that may arise during the purchase of a home. Ultimately, it is very beneficial to own a home. It can be one of the most rewarding purchases you can make.

PERCEPTION IS REALITY

The general perception in the marketplace is that a real estate agent just locates your next home, or places a sign in your yard and their work stops there. Another perception is that all it takes is a simple home search or task to get the job done. Oftentimes pre-scripted television shows detail how a real estate agent drives around in a fancy car showing luxurious homes to home buyers. The cameramen follow them around and show the good and bad reactions of the potential home buyers. Most of the time these buyers were coached by the producer to react a certain way, or to cause an issue that keeps the viewer glued to the TV.

While this may make for good television, my experience in the real estate industry has identified this as false. Truth be told, there are many issues that can come up during the home buying process. Make no mistake what is shown on TV is not always factual. If the only thing a real estate agent had to do was locate your next dream home with a simple search, then quite honestly, there would be no need for real estate agents. It would be a simple process of the buyer looking online to locate their next house. A REALTOR® should guide you properly through each step of the process and explain what is necessary to get the deal accomplished. Sounds simple right? You wouldn't believe how many real estate agents fail at this task.

Sometimes I am told that my profession as a REALTOR® is part psychologist and part sales professional. This is primarily because whether you are buying or selling a home, it is probably one of the most stressful situations you can be in. One of the most important things you should have when buying or selling real estate is the right professional working for you. This is a decision that should not be taken lightly. Having a reliable expert handling your buying/selling deal can make or break the situation. And when it comes to where you will live next, you don't want to make the wrong decision in choosing the wrong professional. This can make for a real bad situation that nobody wants to be in.

I have always considered myself a people person. I love hearing about what others are doing in life and how their days are spent moving towards their goal(s). When I meet with a potential new client, I enjoy asking the right questions about what they are looking for in their next home. This is quite contrary to salespeople who just show up and announce the great things they have done and how wonderful they are. This more often than not turns off the potential client.

Nobody wants to hear how great someone thinks they are. People want to know what you are going to do for them. They want to see a plan of action. They want to know that you will have their best interests placed front and center all the time. When I meet with a potential home buyer, I ask questions that will help me locate the best property for their needs. I ask questions such as, what area they are looking at, do they have things that they must have in their next home, etc. All these elements tie into a very positive experience with them. A real estate professional should always ask more than they tell. You wouldn't believe how many real estate agents are at an appointment with a potential client where they throw out everything about themselves, or what they have done in the past. This is not what potential clients want to hear.

People like talking about themselves. Asking the right questions not only shows that you honestly care about what their needs are, but it also shows that you care about getting the right information so that you can work better for them. Have you ever been to a restaurant where the server took your order without writing anything down only to have an error or two in your order? Writing things down not only shows you are interested in the other person's needs, it also forces you to listen more and speak less. I have heard of some buyer agents showing their clients properties that don't even match any of the criteria that the client wants. This is due to the professional not listening to the client from the beginning.

THE BAR NEEDS TO BE RAISED

There are many reasons why people get into the real estate profession. It could be for the potential of the paycheck or the alleged glamour the TV shows portray. It could be that they love houses, or want a more flexible schedule that this type of career offers. There could be an even more genuine reason than that. It could be that they love interacting with people and help solve problems in the real estate industry.

One of my strongest reasons for becoming a REALTOR® was the fact that I love homes and I love interacting with people. I like the challenge(s) that real estate throws at me and I love seeing sellers and buyers exchange house keys; it is a very powerful moment. I know not just from professional experience, but also from personal experience that purchasing a home is a huge event for most people and it should not be taken lightly.

I am proud to say that I am a home owner. I remember those days when my wife and I closed on our homes; we were like kids in a candy store and could not move our items into our new home fast enough. There is something magical about moving into a home. After all, it is where you rest your head at night and take a break from the world. If you have children, a home is where they grow up. It's where you grow older with your significant other. It's where you detox with a good book and a glass of wine. A home is where you share memories with friends and family. I don't think you could buy any other item and have the same feeling. You can go out and purchase a car and the new car feeling and smell wears off after a month. You could purchase a boat and maybe put it in the water twice a year, unless you're an avid boater. Most aren't, a house can provide years and even generations of good memories for those that live in it and for those who visit the home. A home can also be an income generating asset; in some cases creating more wealth than the stock market and with more certainty.

It's no surprise that houses are an emotional purchase, which drives people to be inspired. It can also drive people to insanity, if the process is not done right, or the wrong professional was hired to work with the buyer or seller. This is why I am thrilled that every day I am a part of that experience for someone. Creating less stressful situations is something a real estate professional should have on top of their mind for their clients.

I wrote this book to share with you some of the things a real estate transaction can throw at you and to share a little bit more of me with you. Also, to make sure that you have better information should you have to make a decision on hiring someone to help you buy or sell a home. I also wrote this book because there is a myth that real estate agents really do not do that much, except list a house and make a commission. This couldn't be farther from the truth! In this book you will learn more about what a REALTOR® does, plus some real world scenarios that would probably make your head spin. Real estate is one of those types of industries where anything can happen. And that's why I stand proud to be a successful REALTOR®.

LIFE AS A REALTOR®

I have to say that it has been a roller coaster of a ride as a REALTOR®. I have seen a lot of things happen from people losing self-control when deals fall apart, to people crying because they received keys to their dream home. It is probably one of the most emotional industries I have been in. And for this, I will continue to hustle and grind to make my clients' dreams come true, all while making sure none of my clients get a bad experience at the closing table.

Many industries don't even come close to what a career in real estate can offer. Sure there are highs and lows, but if done right, there are more highs than low's because that is where the skills and experience come in to play. In fact, most inexperienced, or ill prepared real estate agents, quit the business due to not being able to handle the low or stressful times. They go from one deal to another with large gaps in between of little or no sales. They also tend to only think of their potential commission and therefore add stress to the client. This should not be! True professionals will divert the stress on our clients and handle it. An experienced agent will be able to accomplish this.

A true professional will work hard and smart for their clients to make sure things go smooth and to intercept issues before they arise in a deal.

I hope you enjoy reading this book as much as I enjoyed writing it. Now let's dive into the content.

DIFFERENCES BETWEEN A REALTOR® AND A REAL ESTATE AGENT

Many people do not know that there is a difference between a REALTOR® and a real estate agent. Real estate is a big deal to many people. A home could be the biggest purchase of someone's life. Hiring a professional should not be taken lightly. With that said, you want to know that the person you are looking to hire to find your next home, or sell an existing one, is professional and understanding of your needs. In the real estate industry, one mistake could cost you thousands of dollars at the closing table. While many people use the term REALTOR® loosely, there is a very distinct difference between a REALTOR® and a Real Estate Agent.

Here are some differences between a REALTOR® and a Real Estate Agent:

1.   A REALTOR® has a fiduciary responsibility to you that goes beyond the standard practice.

While all Real Estate Agents are supposed to practice professionally and ethically in your best interest, a REALTOR® upholds that responsibility and then some. A REALTOR® belongs to the National Association of REALTORS® and follows a whole other Code of Ethics. The consequences for not following the code of ethics are steep if a violation occurs. This means that you will typically receive more professional service and effort form a REALTOR® than a standard Real Estate Agent.

2.   Real Estate Moves Fast; Regulations change often.

Many things can change in the real estate industry in terms of regulations and various other guidelines. A REALTOR® has their finger on the pulse of what is changing and how it affects their clients. I recently had a client who was able to receive a tax break on their transfer tax after the sale of their home, due to a new guideline that was released. It is important to know what is happening in real estate.

3.   Knowledge of pricing and selling a home.

There is more to finding value to a home than by searching zillow. While pricing a home can be somewhat of an art and science combined, a REALTOR® knows what your local markets are doing. A REALTOR® has access to much more information than a standard real estate agent relying on just comparables to come up with the price. A REALTOR® can see the upswings in your area and can even look beyond the comparables to see where your neighborhood sales are heading.

4.   REALTORS® follow a stronger Code of Ethics.

While many real estate professionals aim to follow a basic

code of ethics that was maybe implemented by their state or company, a REALTOR® upholds a whole other Code Of Ethics that ensure that your fiduciary duties are met. Like I said earlier in this chapter, when you are making the biggest purchase of your lifetime, or selling your biggest item in your life, you want to know that the professional you hired for the transaction is competent and upholds a much higher Code of Ethics than that of a standard agent. This is not to say that all real estate agents are horrible. It means that hiring a true REALTOR® can make or break your next purchase or home sale. Why settle for someone who does the bare minimum to become an agent?

A REALTOR® and a real estate agent are both licensed to practice real estate. However, a REALTOR® is a real estate agent with higher levels of certification and is typically a member of more than one professional association. They are held to a much higher ethical standard through their REALTOR® associations. REALTORS® are typically more productive and successful at practicing real estate, because of their commitment to the industry. For a seller, or buyer, this provides a much greater opportunity to reach a larger network, compared to an agent that is just doing the basics to get by with their license.

5.   A REALTOR® can help find you the right home; while looking for pros and cons.

When you are looking for a home to purchase or lease, it can get emotional. Oftentimes, a home buyer will get emotionally attached to a property. While this is certainly not a bad thing, it does however, impair some judgment should something go south with negotiations, or even at the closing table. Your REALTOR® is highly educated to know how to deal with the ups and downs of real estate and can be a reliable third party negotiator working in your favor. A standard real estate agent is not as highly trained to deal with certain obstacles that may happen during the process.

6.   Contracts and negotiations can change often.

A REALTOR® often times will know about changes in contracts ahead of time BEFORE they go into effect. Most of these changes are shared with the various professional associations a REALTOR® is a member of. This is a huge benefit to the clients a REALTOR® serves. Having a more in-depth look at where contracts and guidelines are heading could benefit the client more than the basic information a real estate agent has.

These are just some of the differences between a REALTOR® and a Real Estate Agent. Some people have told me that a REALTOR® seems to take their career more serious. Of course, keep in mind that you also have to personally like the person you are hiring! You won't get far if you are not getting along with your professional, or they are not providing you the communication you deserve throughout the process.

A REALTOR® can bring more to the table and provide a higher level of service to their clients. They often come with better negotiation skills, experience with difficult transactions, and have more skin in the game as it financially costs more to be a REALTOR®. This means a higher commitment to providing you the best service possible. I do forewarn though, you should make sure even the REALTOR® asks you the right questions and addresses your needs properly.

The first step in whether you are buying or selling a home, besides making sure finances are in order, is to make sure you work with a REALTOR® who will share the differences above with you. If you are at that stage, then please contact me today and let's talk real estate!

For more information or to reach out to Jason Gelios; Please visit: www.ItsAllAboutTheRealEstate.com.

BEWARE OF THE AFA AGENT

We talked about the various differences between a REALTOR® and a real estate agent. Now let's talk about what an AFA agent is. You may not have heard of this term, but I can tell you almost everyone knows this type of agent.

The AFA agent is the Average-Frustrated-Agent! This type of agent is a virus and spreads like crazy in the real estate industry. For every one good REALTOR®, there are ten of these types of agents!

This type of agent exhibits many symptoms that kill deals, tick people off and stress out buyers and sellers even more. You can typically find this agent hanging out by the water cooler in the office daily. They pray that a hot lead will call in and hire them to locate, or sell a home. They go to all the office parties held by the broker to 'escape' from the reality of having to go out and actually find or earn business. It is rare that I see top producers hanging out at the office daily, unless they are running a team. Even then, they are usually out networking or meeting with clients.

After meeting many of these agents, I am here to tell you that they make things a lot worse in a deal. How do they do that you ask? Because they are AFA agents; they tend to do the bare minimum in terms of communication with their clients, or other parties involved such as agents, lenders, etc. Even worse, they may not even do the minimum! They often waste time and act so desperate to get their next commission check that they will usually cross over the ethical line. They will put their own interests first, instead of looking out for the best interest of their clients. Get my drift? They will do questionable things to close a deal, all while not caring what position they put their clients in. This is the type of agent you want to avoid at all costs.

So how do you avoid them? Well, if you do not know the agent personally, you could interview and ask for their track record. Are they familiar with your area and what has sold recently? Do they know what properties in your area have gone pending offers? What properties are actively listed? Do they have a strong online presence and networking consistently? Did they bring a marketing plan to show you what they will do to sell your home?

An AFA agent or Average Frustrated Agent will 'wing it' and only try to provide you a suggested selling price based on their own personal opinion, not fact. This frustrates not only the home owner looking to sell their home, but other professionals that base their decision on facts not fiction.

Remember, AFA agents won't do much work. They just get by long enough until they decide to quit the business. Of course this is after they have wreaked havoc all over the place!

WHEN LISTING AGENTS REVEAL TOO MUCH INFORMATION

I was working with a buyer client who was looking for a home and wanted a nice size ranch that required very little work to move in. We looked at multiple properties in and around the desired area to provide my client a better idea of what was available and to confirm the purchase was a solid choice. We located a nice ranch home that fit their needs and we decided to write an offer. Upon the receipt of our offer by the listing agent, I noticed that she pretty much revealed her clients' willingness to accept a strong offer. The agent had gone on to share with me details about her seller client. That was strike one. We were anticipating a positive response and got the formal acceptance within a day. I had no doubts about my clients' offer, because the listing agent had provided too many details to me. A listing agent should never reveal too much to a buyer's agent, unless the seller demands the listing agent do so.

As we proceeded throughout the process, there were several moments the listing agent (who represents the seller) was a little too anxious about getting the deal done. While we were moving along faster than the normal time frame, this agent was very eager to close on the deal to where it actually frustrated everyone involved on the buying side. As we made our way to closing the deal, it had occurred to me that this listing agent was desperate to close this deal to have money for the holidays. While some could empathize with this agent, I find that this is no excuse to jeopardize a client's position just because it benefits the agents' self interests first. This type of behavior could have pushed away the buyer or affected negotiations during the process. A real estate agent should 'always' put their clients' best interests first, regardless of their own financial situation or position.

MANY REAL ESTATE AGENTS QUIT; HERE IS WHY

Let's be brutally honest here. Many real estate agents don't stick around long enough to do well, or provide the 'experience' that a client needs or deserves. Nor do they go the extra mile to be successful, or provide the expertise a client demands. You might be thinking that it is bold of me to say this, but I have some facts to back up my statement. *FACT: Did you know over 85% of all real estate agents exit the industry within the first year? One does not have to look far to see laziness in the real estate industry, or any other industry for that matter. I wish this was not the case, but it is.

Being a real estate agent requires a lot of work and know how of industry and market standards. We are all aware of someone who is in customer service that does the bare minimum to get by. After all, have you ever been in a store and walked by several employees that flat out ignore you? This happens to me often, and I am a pretty big guy. It's pretty hard to miss me. Yet so many people sign up with a discounted real estate agent expecting great things, only to get exactly what they pay for- garbage service compiled with garbage communication, or none at all! It truly is a fact that you get what you pay for when looking for a real estate professional. I told you this Chapter would be brutally honest.

*Source: NAR

It's necessary though.

To be successful at real estate, an individual has to give it their all. They have to be there for their client when they need them and they have to stay up-to-date with all the latest trends, market information and marketing tactics that a client needs and deserves. They have to put the clients first and have empathy. Clients deserve better. Considering purchasing or selling a home is one of the biggest transactions in someone's life. Yet when you look at how many agents get into the business every year vs. how many of them quit after the same year, it is no surprise why many people view real estate agents as terrible or incompetent. A good REALTOR® will abide by a higher standard and hopefully change your perception of them through honest, hard working efforts that a buyer or seller deserve.

DISCOUNTED AGENTS EQUAL DISCOUNTED SERVICE

There are real estate agents out in the industry that offer a discounted service for home sellers. A home owner looking to possibly sell their home cheap can hire a discounted agent to get their house listed on the MLS and maybe put a sign in the yard. That, unfortunately, is where service stops. With a discount agent and service, your house will be on the MLS with limited coverage and limited service. Even the contract they have you sign states limited service. In my opinion, this discounted service offering is just one step above selling by owner. Even with this discounted service, the homeowner has to field any potential buyers and handle the transaction themselves. So why have a discounted real estate agent list your home? It makes no sense to have a discounted agent somewhat handle one of your biggest transactions in your life. As I mentioned earlier in this book, buying or selling real estate is a big deal that should not be taken lightly. Discounted agent's equal discounted service.

I want to share with you the real estate agent that will discount their commission too easily to gain a home sellers agreement to sell their home. This is just a regular real estate agent with no faith in what they do, or offer. This is often an agent that has no real experience or confidence in the real estate industry. The minute a homeowner mentions a discount, they drop it fast to gain the business.

What you have to ask yourself is if an agent will discount their commission that fast how will they handle negotiations for your home? Will they reveal that a seller is desperate to sell? I see this all the time on the MLS. SELLER MOTIVATED! If I am on the buying side I see this as an invitation to write up a lower offer if my clients have an interest in the home.

Discounted agents should not be hired in my opinion. They are like a cancer that infects sellers and ultimately cause more stress than a homeowner needs or deserves. No home seller should have to deal with this just to save some money. Discounted agents often cost a homeowner a lot more money due to poor service, lack of communication, time wasted and poor negotiations.

CREATE MORE VALUE THAN WHAT IS EXPECTED

One day I was driving by a house with a For Sale By Owner sign off the road. As I followed the beautiful subdivision road to the well-kept landscaping in front of this ranch style home, I noticed that another agent left his 'postcard' on the front door handle. As I was approaching the door, I was thinking of what I was bringing to the table. I had crafted and designed a full fledged FSBO folder with tips on selling by owner. It is not only a value packed folder FOR THE SELLER, but it is also a powerful marketing tool that positions myself as the expert. Now I ask you, if you were a seller and homeowner coming home to a postcard or a value packed folder with advice, which would you keep? Exactly. Providing value is so important because people don't care about your postcard. They care about the value proposition you offer. In other words, what is in it for them? Should I devote my time to this person?

While offering value sounds so simple, why is it most professionals do not offer it? Why is it that most marketing pieces are self absorbed and describe everything about the professional with a 'call me' statement? Do people react well to this type of marketing piece? I doubt it. By putting myself into the person's shoes I am trying to connect with, I set myself up for success. Sure, nobody hit's every ball they swing for, but I guarantee you, I will hit more balls or successes by connecting with those I want to do business with compared to someone who is less prepared and does the absolute minimum. Personalizing every interaction or providing something the potential client wants or needs will always work better than a generic marketing piece that is not valuable.

DUE DILIGENCE IS KEY

There was one particular deal where I was representing my buyers and we located a nice home for them that would match the needs of their family. We went over all the specifics and what they were looking to offer. I presented an aggressive offer which included the furniture that was in the home along with some other items that were requested by my buyers. And because the home needed some work and tender loving care, we were able to present a below asking price offer. We were pleasantly told the offer was accepted. Everything seemed smooth with the process including a decent inspection that met the satisfaction of the buyers. I was conducting my research on the home and noticed that the tax amount seemed very high compared to other homes in the area. Armed with this information, I needed to find out what was going on. Come to find out, the city was actually taxing an extra piece of land with the home my buyers were purchasing. While this was a simple issue to fix, it was not discovered by the seller's title company. You see, this is one of the reasons I set my home buyers up with a title company that represents them. This is considered a split closing. Had I not done the research to make sure everything was where it should be most likely this would have been caught just days before closing and have stalled the signing. Another issue that arose with this house was that the seller had let the power go and the vacant home was now without power. Worse yet, it was a week where we were seeing, or feeling I should say, zero below winter weather! This prompted a phone call from me to the seller's agent and basically advising him to turn the power back on to avoid damage to the home. Could you imagine showing up for the final walkthrough, which I recommend on every deal, and seeing pipes burst with what could be catastrophic damage everywhere? These are the types of things that a great REALTOR® can assist a home buyer with. And unfortunately not all issues like these are caught in time. This can cause even more grief.

Sometimes I am told that my profession as a REALTOR® is part psychologist and part real estate agent. This is primarily because whether you are buying or selling a home, it is probably one of the most stressful situations you can be in apart from divorce or personal injury. The most important thing is that to have the right professional on your side that can make or break your deal. And when it comes to where you will live next, you don't want to make the wrong decision by choosing the wrong professional.

THE MLS IS NOT EVERYTHING AND HERE IS WHY

There is a misconception that if you put a property on the MLS (Multiple Listing Service) and you upload some photos, you will automatically get buyers swarming to the home. While this may get some buyers to see your property, this is not the magic formula. Truth be told, it takes a strong marketing mind and consistency to create the sale of a home. The MLS is one of the many tools a good REALTOR® will use to attract buyers to your home, but certainly not the only one. Top producers tend to always be networking and building connections so that when they do have a home to sell, it gets shared more intimately and therefore gains more interest. There are some services out there that advertise that they will list your property on the MLS for a nominal fee. While this is true, that typically is not effective. Don't get me wrong, anything has the potential to work once, but you don't want to pay the fee and gamble with the sale of your home. These one-time MLS fee services often stop offering you assistance once they upload your property. Do you really want your house uploaded and forgotten about? Do you know who will be walking through your home? Often times this presents safety issues because the buyers are not pre-screened, or qualified.

A home sale or purchase can be one of the biggest transactions in most people's lives. Why bet on low service offerings? REALTORS® can offer you full service from listing your home with greater exposure to taking care of showings and making sure only qualified buyers are viewing your property. Think about the security of knowing prescreened buyers are in your home with a licensed agent. To have the expertise and knowledge of a REALTOR® is what makes the process much simpler when you sell a home. Never leave anything to chance and never ever put security on the back burner when you have a house on the market. Whether you are selling by owner, or with an agent, make sure that safety and security measures are in place.

MARKETING PLAN

If you sat down with several agents and asked each one if they had a plan to market your home for the most exposure and potential buyers, probably 4 out of 5 would look at you like an alien. Marketing plans are huge, because your property is a product that a real estate professional should be selling. Smart, marketing savvy professionals should have a marketing plan. A marketing plan can be as simple as a few things showing what they are, or how they intend to market your property. It doesn't have to be anything elaborate, just a plan of action. It should also be backed up by facts and numbers from the neighborhood.

If you are meeting with a real estate professional to list your home and they do not share a marketing plan that is in tune with the year you are in, do not hire them!

As a professional REALTOR®, I network daily with other top producers and professionals to ensure that when they have a property for sale, or I present a property to the market, it gets maximum effort, not just an addition to the MLS. I often work consistently so that when I do have a property to sell, it gets a lot of eyes on it even before it hits the MLS and other various websites. So my point here is make sure you work with someone who does more than just put a sign in your yard and post your property to the MLS.

VIDEO MARKETING

I am an advocate of video marketing to sell homes and create interest. As a matter of fact, if done right, video can dramatically increase the amount of buyers who may have an interest in the home. Multiple buyers mean a higher offer price and less hassles throughout the process. Here is an interesting statistic from NAR (National Association of REALTORS®): *Homes that use video in their marketing sell four times as fast as those who don't. Pretty interesting right? Yet so many home sellers make the choice of hiring an agent that does not use video. Maybe they are hiring an agent in the family. Maybe the home seller doesn't think video is important. Maybe the seller is worried people will judge the home in a negative way, or people won't view the home if they saw it online.

Truth is, video can present the house in a positive light and create more demand. People will be begging to see it! This is smarter marketing. Think about it; would YOU rather scroll through poorly taken pictures of a house, or view a professionally created video as if you are there? I guarantee you if two homes were for sale on the same street and one used video while the other did not, the one that has a professional video will get way more interest and possibly a higher offer price!

CREATING VIDEO FOR BUSINESS

I am a huge fan of creating video content, because it is the easiest way for people to consume valuable information. While some people do still read articles and books, video is a faster and easier way for busy people to digest information. Most people are busy, they find it easier to

*Source: NAR

consume a quick video or two on the go. Being right there on someone's smart phone or tablet while they are waiting at a doctor's office, on a plane, or wherever is why I dedicate myself to answering questions people have to recording and sharing my quick real estate tips online. I do all of this so that people feel comfortable with one of the most emotional transactions they will ever experience. So I implore you to read through this book and really take in the information and life experiences that it provides so that not only will you have a more accurate view of what a successful real estate agent does, but also the value that one can bring to the table. Now notice I wrote PROFESSIONAL. Like anything else in life, there are poorly made videos too. A poorly made video might as well be not made at all, because it has a negative effect on how the property looks. However, a poorly made video is not worse than not having one at all. I have known people that have recorded a whole video that probably would have benefited the viewer, only to find out they deleted it, or never shared it to begin with.

I can remember back when I was a high school student I had a keen interest in video. I would hang out for two hours or more in the film class while we created content for the school channel. We would invite the sports teams and other people planning events to be the 'talent' in our shows. They would share what was going on in the school and what sporting events were coming up. The students and staff really liked the videos we produced, because they brought value and information to those that watched.

Let's flash forward many years to my real estate career. Ever since I started using video for not just my listings, but for sharing valuable content to an audience, I have received a very good response to the content. More importantly, the houses sold faster! If you want to grab and keep people's attention, you need to provide them something that they find valuable. It is very important to also stay in people's minds, because at the end of the day this helps with getting attention on a house I am trying to sell. How is this a benefit to the seller you ask? I create the medium to where I have people's attention and then I can share houses that I have on the market. While the MLS pushes the house out there to multiple websites as well, there are so many homes on the market. Agents like to see a fellow agent sharing a house they have for sale on an interesting video medium. Most people pay more attention to videos than an article, or home searches sent by an agent.

BUYERS AND SELLERS NEED TO BE TAKEN CARE OF

I was working with a young family that was making a move from a tiny 2 bedroom apartment to a 2,000 sq ft home in a beautiful neighborhood. This was their first home and they were using a lot of their savings for the down payment. I had taken them out and shown them multiple houses until arriving to the one that they would soon fall in love with.

We walked through the home and imagined how they would live in the home. Where would their furniture go? Where would the kids play? How would they finish the basement? You get the idea. We talked about our negotiation strategy and we ended up sending over our offer that same night.

Upon our offer getting accepted, we lined up the inspector for the home. As we got further through the process, we noticed some things had happened on the seller's side to the home. We noticed some electrical fixtures were not working. The furnace had a broken pipe that was leaking into the basement and the electrical meter was pulled off the side of the home. All of these things were adding up to a lot of stress for my buyers. At one point, I thought the deal was going to die and my buyers would have to back out of this house. Thankfully, things worked out in the end. We were able to have the seller make these repairs and bring the house back to the way it appeared during the initial showing.

The closing was to take place at the seller's business office and I lined up my preferred title company to represent the buyer's side. In real estate, this is called a split closing. I arrived at the office for the closing, along with the title closer, buyer clients, and the lender for this particular transaction. We made our way to the conference room and the title closer started the signing for my buyers in an effort to save time. After about a half an hour, the seller's title closer came in late. Not only did she come in late to a prescheduled closing, she had many of the numbers wrong on her settlement statement for the seller. Typically, this is a big red flag during a closing. This also paints a not so professional picture of the closer. But in this case, we decided to wait until she balanced her numbers.

After the seller's title company had figured out her numbers and satisfied both the seller and my buyer, we noticed yet another issue that would end up having us close in escrow. There was a lien on the title that was allegedly cleared up, but was not. This was primarily on the seller's side of the transaction. While both title companies scrambled to make it right, we determined that this needed to close in escrow with a two day deadline to get the title cleared. What was even more interesting to me, however, was that the seller said it would be easier to have only one title company close both sides. Why this was interesting to me is that what if these multiple issues were not corrected and my buyers signed off without having someone truly on their side? You see, this is why I automatically have a preferred title company represent my buyers in a transaction. You want that representation on your side when you sign closing documents for a home.

One of the most important things to look out for when choosing who will help you find your next dream home is to make sure they know how to guide you through the process.

It is not enough to just choose a real estate agent, but to really know who you are hiring. Would an inexperienced real estate agent know to have a split closing with a title closer on the buyer's side? Would they know that certain things can happen and that you can close in escrow to fix the issue? While there were many issues that arose, I was able to be the non-emotional third party that was involved in making sure everything eventually closed.

I'm proud to say that the family is still enjoying the home they purchased and they are creating great memories that will last a lifetime.

NETWORKING IS A WAY OF LIFE

All good REALTORS® that I know network with other professionals. It means the difference between an inexperienced agent, versus an experienced one. I always network with other top producers in my field, because agents like to help one another. They also like to do business with agents they like. How does this help you the home seller or buyer? This could mean a better experience through the process as agents communicate smoothly with each other. It could also mean your offer being recommended over another agent who may have a reputation of being difficult to work with. A good agent that networks effectively can also get you even more exposure on your home sale through relationships that were built. Unfortunately, less tenured agents do not network well. They may show up to some events and hand out business cards awkwardly. They may even go to so many networking events, but not focus on actually selling homes, therefore not having anything to promote. This can have a negative effect on the home they are trying to sell. The importance of networking should be a part of every good agent's marketing plan.

ENJOYING THE DAILY GRIND

Real estate is hard work. It takes a certain someone to do this job. You have to be able to handle the stressful situations and the barrage of information that can come your way. Often times, people ask me how I work so hard and keep up with the fast paced real estate career I chose? They wonder how I manage to keep tabs on everything and still be effective and valuable to my clients.

The answer to this question is very simple.
I LOVE REAL ESTATE.

It doesn't get much simpler than that. I love the hustle. I love how real estate can be challenging and no one day is the same. I love the look on someone's face when they receive their keys to their new home. Sure, I could say that I make a great living. But honestly, it is not one hundred percent the reason why I chose to market and sell homes. It is the experience.

No matter how many clients I work with on any given day, I hustle to get in front of sellers and buyers. Whether it is social media, traditional marketing, or networking, I make it my mission to be front and center to maximize exposure for my clients. This type of hustle has not only provided me some pretty good opportunities, but also has provided my clients opportunity as well. Whether I use social media, or networking events to be in front of my network, it is very important to work smart, as well as it is hard to provide the best value possible for those that choose to work with me.

Now you may be thinking that I think I sound better than most real estate agents. Well, you would be right. The facts are in the numbers. Most real estate agents do not work hard enough to make a difference to their clients. They meet with a potential client and talk all about the MLS and that is about it. Typically, that is all a potential client/homeowner knows is value is the MLS. Even worse, they have no written or digital marketing plan or plan of action. They suggest you sell your house at some low ball price to get it to sell faster, while you lose money in the deal. Does this really happen you ask? Yes! It does. All the time unprepared real estate agents go out and only push the home seller to list the home at a low price to gain a lot of interest. Do you see any value in that? I didn't think so. Why work with someone who does the minimum? Do they deserve your business?

Chances are you are reading this book thinking that other agents don't have a book. If you want someone serious about real estate, ask them the questions necessary to make the right decision. Do not just choose a family member who happens to be an agent. Do not gamble with what could be the biggest decision in your life. Choose a serious real estate professional that will get the job done, or lose possible thousands of dollars to inexperience.

I remember first thinking about becoming a REALTOR®. My sister was working at an in-house title company that was a part of a real estate office. I mentioned how my kids were a little older and that I was getting tired of corporate America and their lack of respect for employees. I scheduled a sit down with a fiery energetic woman who was the Office Manager and VP in charge of agent development. As she was going over the many benefits of what being a real estate agent offers, I could not help but feel this was the better side of the real estate transaction for me. I had been on the mortgage side of things and wanted a change. I always knew I could sell and market things and even had the accolades from prior endeavors to back it up. I was ready to move onto bigger and better things. I was ready to make a move and finally sell something that I was very interested in, homes. A house can be personal and unique. There is an emotional connection with a home and its owner(s). It is a decision that I have not regretted since.

One of my daily philosophies is to make every day count. Never let yourself or anyone else waste your valuable time. On that same note, try not to waste anyone else's time either. While this seems like easy advice to follow, unfortunately, I see people wasting time every day. Average real estate agents hang out and gossip when top agents are busy working and being productive. They are the ones that party too much and share that on their social media. Why would anyone want to do business with agents that do not work or connect with their network on a regular basis? I know this may sound a little cruel, but I can tell you this happens.

People want to work with professionals who work and hustle. If I cannot deliver great results, then I have failed as your go-to real estate professional. My crazy work ethic is why I push myself harder than most to be successful in my career and life. Nobody wants' to be average, yet so many people settle for it. When starting my career in real estate, I made it my mission to be excellent and to help as many people as possible. My daily goal was and is to help as many people get what they want, therefore, success for me has followed.

SELLING A HOME BY OWNER; A GOOD IDEA?

This section is probably going to hit hard for some people who have maybe had some success in selling a home themselves. While some people have had success selling a home on their own, it rarely happens. After all, there are so many items to cover during a real estate transaction that it entails more than just putting out a yard sign and finding a buyer on your own. It takes research and time to sell a home by owner. This is not my personal opinion, I have some facts to back it up.

*It is estimated that over 87% of all home owners that sell for sale by owner end up hiring a real estate agent anyway. While there are some people that have the gumption to sell their home on their own, most don't have what it takes. Why do the majority of the homes put on the market never end up selling by owner? My personal theory is that the homeowner/seller didn't do the research needed to know ALL aspects of selling a home on their own. It could also be that the home was not properly presented to the potential buyers looking for a home. Things like pricing, description of the home, pictures, etc could also have played a factor.

You may be thinking that this sounds harsh, but I assure you I have seen homeowners put a sign in their yard, have an open house and not even know what the next step would be should someone present an interest/offer. This is where the research up front could have helped them be more prepared. I feel a homeowner can absolutely sell a home on their own, provid-ed they do the research BEFORE they put the 'By Owner'

*Source: NAR

house for sale sign in the front yard, or upload the property to the internet. It takes a huge amount of work to sell a house. If selling a house were as easy as putting it on a couple of internet websites and adding the sign in the yard, then real estate agents would be out of commission. Many times a homeowner feels that a real estate agent just comes out, puts the sign out and includes the property on the MLS not knowing that there are many more aspects and pieces that have to be put together on the back end for a house to be highly visible. Often times, it takes a lot of time and effort to sell a home. You have to have a great network and many resources to properly sell a home at a great price.

A homeowner selling on their own relies on two pieces of marketing. They rely on the yard sign, which usually has no information on it with a faded phone number, or a popular real estate website. To be brutally honest here, many real estate agents won't even bring a buyer to a FSBO (For Sale By Owner) home. It just doesn't happen often.

You may have read that last part and are thinking that I am against a homeowner selling their home by owner. Truth be told, I feel anyone can sell a house if they do the right homework and have the right advice presented to them. I am simply encouraging people to know how much it takes and to get the information upfront before they put the home up for sale by owner. The last thing you want to have happen is not knowing how to go forward and lose thousands of dollars in negotiations, because you do not come across professionally by not knowing the process.

Side note: When I work with home buyers, I will show them all houses for sale based on their criteria, even For Sale By Owner homes. Make sure you are not missing out on these homes.

I will show my buyer clients homes, regardless of how they are for sale. One of the main reasons an agent will not show a home for sale by owner, is because most agents assume that the homeowner hates agents and/or they won't pay a buyer's agent fee. Even worse, they don't think of the client's needs first! While many homes sold by owner would happily pay a commission to just the buyer's agent, many agents assume that they won't. Imagine a home that is for sale by owner being passed up by an agent that has qualified buyers. Could you imagine working with a real estate agent who will not show you a For Sale By Owner home because of assumption, or even fear? Would you not want to see a home because the agent would not show it to you? Make sure that your buyers' agent shows you all properties for sale, or at least makes an effort to reach out to homes sold by owner on your behalf, unless it is documented that they will not work with a REALTOR®. This is usually not the case.

When it comes to assumptions that buyers' agents may have, there is a myth out there that For Sale By Owners, or as I like to call them Unrepresented Sellers, are not willing to work with an agent or REALTOR®. Many Real Estate Agents do not show buyers the homes that are for sale by owner out of fear or a notion that they will not receive a commission should their buyer decide to choose the home listed with a REALTOR®. I would like to say that this myth is mostly false. However, it isn't totally. Most Real Estate professionals that I talk to simply drive right by and ignore the home that is for sale by owner. This is very sad. The fact that a typical real estate agent would ignore an unrepresented seller at the expense of their client is very discouraging. When you work with a REALTOR®, they should make sure your best interests are met. As a REALTOR® myself, I always know the area and what is for sale either by owner or by another listing agent.

Having had the pleasure of speaking to many For Sale By Owners, often times the owner does not know why the agent drove right by their home after showing a home on their street. Nor do they understand why the agents simply don't make a phone call and ask them if the homeowner would consider working with the agent to show a client a home that could potentially meet their needs. Not only is this bad practice by the agent, it is straight up rude. As a REALTOR® myself, I will call a For Sale By Owner and ask them about their home. I would ask them if they would allow me to show the home to my client and if there is an interest, would they work with me. What most real estate agents fail to see is that most homeowner would not mind paying commission to a buyer's agent, because it would still be less than paying a buyers and selling agent.

If you are looking to purchase a home, please make sure you work with someone that has YOUR best interest' front and center. If not, you could lose the chance to see your next dream home, because the wrong professional ignored homes sold by owner.

We talked about how some buyers' agents behave towards a for sale by owner home. Now let's take a look at some staggering statistics about selling a home by owner. *89% of homes sold in 2017 were sold by a real estate professional. An estimated 88% of homes were found by a real estate professional. These are overwhelming results that show that working with a professional REALTOR® can provide better benefit to the client. Now, I certainly don't discourage someone from selling a home by owner. It may even work for some. But there are some things that the home seller needs to know before tackling this process. There is more to selling a home than putting a sign on the front lawn and distributing some flyers.

If you have the time, money, resources, knowledge of contracts, negotiation skills, ability to leave emotions out of the equation, signs, flyers, marketing, online exposure over a wide reach, open house materials, etc., then I encourage

*Source: NAR

you to sell by owner. This section is not designed to dissuade you from selling by owner. It is a reality check that simply reminds those looking to sell by owner to do the research, so that you are better prepared to handle the process from start to finish.

As a REALTOR®, I get the pleasure of meeting many types of people who have different life goals and objectives. This allows me to learn what their wants and needs are from their home sale. I especially love working with 'For Sale By Owners' or as I like to call them, Unrepresented Sellers. Unrepresented sellers know what they want and where they need to be to consider selling their home. While most of the time they learn the actual figure that the market will pay for, unrepresented sellers are willing to make a change to sell their home at a faster pace with greater effectiveness, because it doesn't matter what price a home seller needs to get, if the market will not pay that price. Of course, this is through the assistance of a REALTOR®.

I have seen it many times where a homeowner has to get a certain price for their home and are oblivious to the fact that the market may not pay that price for the home. The market will pay what the market will pay. A potential home buyer will not pay more for a home simply because the seller has to make a certain amount off of the sale. Market value is determined by factors that are not tied directly to what the seller needs at closing.

You may be at that point where you have attempted to sell your home on your own and have not had much luck. Maybe you realized that it takes a lot more time and effort to manage all aspects of the selling process. It doesn't have to be complicated. Putting your faith into someone who does real estate daily will ease the burden of selling your home. REALTORS® know the ins and outs of real estate and can take care of all the tasks that come with selling a home.

Some homeowners may want to sell their home by owner because they have the time and energy to handle what comes along with the process. There are ways to be effective when selling your home by owner. I have seen many homes that are for sale by owner and not taking care of the little things. What do I mean by this? I have seen for sale signs that have a faded phone number on the sign that cannot be read. I have seen flyer boxes that are empty for several days or even weeks. I have left generic messages with just my name and number only to receive no call back by the owner. How on earth is a potential buyer supposed to see the home, or get more information, if the owner does not even call them back?

If you are going to sell your home by owner, please don't make these mistakes. These small mistakes can cost you a buyer and leave you feeling stressed out even further. The good news is that these mistakes can be avoided now that I shared them in this book.

If you're looking to be successful in selling your home by owner, then be sure to know what you need to know upfront before you put the home online, or put a sign in the yard. Nothing is worse than wasting time trying to sell a home by owner without knowing what has to be done upfront.

Get my free report here.
https://www.itsallabouttherealestate.com/selling-by-owner.html

FINDING OUT ABOUT ISSUES BEFORE THEY WREAK HAVOC

While we talked about how it is possible for a homeowner to sell their home on their own, let's take a look at an issue that arose on one of my deals and how I was able to learn of the issue up front, instead of at the closing.

One of the first things I do when I write an offer, or list a home, is run what is called pre-title. Pre-title is when you have your title company run title to ensure that there are no liens, judgments, or anyone else on the title. This is helpful because it is one way to avoid issues during the process. If an issue does arise, it can be addressed earlier on in the process versus later in the process, which is usually more stressful.

I can remember a specific situation where one of my clients inherited a home from their recently deceased mother. The home had shown only the name of the deceased and was not quit claim deeded to the adult child. This was a simple fix and we were able to get documentation stating the adult child had the right to sell the home.

This is just one of the examples of how your REALTOR® should be working for you. By being proactive, instead of reactive, an issue was fixed before it wreaked havoc and stressed everyone out.

THE POWER OF USING COMING SOON MARKETING

You can leverage the power of coming soon in building a sense of urgency if you have the network and the capability of doing so. When you work with an agent that networks himself and puts himself out there daily, you can have a more marketable property, versus a real estate agent that does not do these things. Truth is, many agents don't have the network and don't constantly work and, therefore, rely on just the MLS to sell your home, or a sign in your yard. This is an old way of thinking and it will not get you the eyes that your property needs to get you the most money for your house sale. I had a transaction where I sold the house with multiple offers in about seven days. I met with the seller and showed the marketing plan that included my thoughts for a profitable sale. One of the things I did was to include video marketing into the marketing plan, as well as creating a sense of urgency with my fellow agents who were working with buyers. So once our agreement was signed and I was able to market the home, I was able to create urgency with other agents who already lined up showings, before the house went live on the MLS. The MLS is such a small part of what goes into selling a home. A good REALTOR® will not just rely on the MLS, but other marketing factors as well. You want to make sure you work with a real estate agent that is connected and has potential buyers before you even show your house to this agent. Because if you don't make the right choice in hiring a real estate agent, it can cost you a lot more in the end, or worse no sale at all.

Now don't get me wrong when you read the above, I still like to use a real estate sign and even flyers and the MLS, but I put most of my focus into video marketing, as well as networking your property to other professionals who have buyers. In most cases this provides a huge sense of urgency and multiple buyers, which can result in multiple offers and a higher offer price for you, the seller. Do not make the mistake of thinking that video marketing is not important, because it is a proven fact that you will have more of an interest and more people coming to see your property with the video than any other marketing tactic. I've seen some agents out there that don't think this is something they should be doing for some of the listings that they have a bit longer on the market. Truth be told they don't want to adapt to something new, or something that they don't understand and unfortunately, this affects the seller's bottom line. Be sure to use all the tools and resources at your disposal to help your home stand out above the rest of the homes in your area for sale. Be sure to do whatever it takes to stand out, because not making a good impression can literally cost you thousands of dollars during negotiations.

GAINING ATTENTION BEFORE HITTING THE MARKET

One day a friend referred me to a young woman who was looking to sell her current home and relocate to a newer home in an area that was more convenient for her and her kids. We went over some things to get her home ready to hit the market successfully. While my client was prepping her home, I was spreading the word about my soon to be listed property. I networked some basic information about the home on and offline to gain some interest before it hit the market. Once my client was ready to put the home on the market, we had been getting some interest in it prior to the launch.

Once this home hit the market, we had a frenzy of showings and conversations, which ultimately led to a multiple offer situation! While this is not common for every house that hits the market, it is much better to gain more attention and interest through coming soon marketing than to not do anything at all. A good agent will do this for their seller client.

If you gain anything from this section, it is that everything should be done to sell a home without dramatically reducing the price right out of the gate. This is what most agents try to do. They brag about selling a home in under thirty days, when in reality they just came out under what the market would have paid for the home. This is not good salesmanship at all.

You want your home to sell expediently without losing on the price. On this same note, however, any amount of marketing and attention will be wasted if a home is priced too high.

Assuming your price is right and agreed upon, you or your agent should utilize the power of coming soon marketing to sell the home; Fast.

YOUR HOME IS NOT AN ASSET

This chapter will have some of you wondering if I really know what I am talking about, but stick with me here. There are a lot of arguments out there about whether or not a home is an asset, or a liability. Many experts claim to have supportive facts and thoughts on both sides of this discussion. Most homeowners will tell you that they see their home as an asset, because it can gain equity. Other homeowners will argue that it is a liability, because if you owe a mortgage on it coupled with the costs of owning and maintaining the home, it is not a real asset. Both sides of this discussion have valid points.

So which side of this discussion is right? Depends on the facts you look at.

One could say it is an asset to the lender, because a homeowner pays the lender to stay in the home. If a homeowner lost their employment, or income source, would your house pay you? I have always viewed a home as an investment in not only yourself, but those you provide the home for. I personally see a house as a liability, but with an appreciation (most times) that benefits the owner. Because unless you sell the home at a profit, you have to pay interest on the money you pull from the house in the form of an equity loan. In a lot of cases you have to pay tax on the gains you made when you sell the house. A house ultimately costs you money and can even work against you, should you not be able to pay the mortgage due to an illness, loss of income or some other tragic event. Even if you have a rental home, it can generate income as well as maintenance costs, although a rental home with a tenant is considered more of an asset than a personal home. While I have provided both sides of this argument, I highly recommend talking to your banker or financial advisor about their opinion on this. But needless to say, most homes are an asset to your banker who holds the lien and not to the home owner.

PROVIDING VALUE TO THOSE WHO NEED IT

Providing value should be the first thing a real estate professional does for someone. It is how you create a wonderful experience for the client while also gaining referrals. People like doing business with people that make them feel less stressed and more informed.

I was introduced to someone who was let go by the agent they were working with. I guess this particular agent stated they didn't have time to view multiple homes and educate the buyer on the process. Imagine that. The buyer had kept her preapproval with the lender that was referred to her by the first agent. We will get back to this point later. Upon getting her information, I was happy to step in and provide the proper experience that this first time buyer deserved.

After confirming her pre-approval letter, we decided to meet at one of the houses she had an interest in. After deciding that a handful of the houses we saw prior were not for her, we found one that appealed to her and her family. I will never forget how new everything was in this house, including newer roof, appliances and paint. I knew this home would be perfect for her and her family, because all the expensive things were updated or replaced. We had a conversation and I drafted up the offer and sent it over. We received the news that our offer was accepted and we were able to move forward towards inspection. While this deal sounded smooth so far, several things popped up. One of the first things that struck me as odd was that when I contacted the lender to let him know we had a signed deal, I was warned that our mutual client had an inspector that killed deals through inspections in order to gain more money.

While this certainly could happen to a buyer, I felt it was odd this lender brought that up to me. Nevertheless, I mentioned this concern to our client who assured me this was not the case. As we progressed further into the deal, I noticed some of the things the lender was doing was not how things should be going. I remember one of the things the lender made a mistake on was that they had misplaced the client's tax returns! This was a huge red flag.

After weeks of this nonsense, my client decided to choose another lender. After extending our closing deadline and moving forward with the new lender, my client closed on her new home. Looking back I had put together some reasons as to why that first lender never worked out. From the beginning, the lender did not have the right program for the buyer and was providing bad advice in hopes to get the clients' credit score up to qualify for the program. When my client looked elsewhere for a mortgage, she found a new lender who had the right program for her.

If it wasn't for the fact that I had been on the mortgage side for years prior to becoming an agent, that first lender probably would have killed the deal and my client would have lost the house and her deposit! It always makes sense to ask a good amount of questions to the lender you choose. You don't want to make a mistake and find out half way through the process of getting a home that you don't qualify for the mortgage. Of course there are situations where you can't help it if an issue arises that is out of your control. Due diligence is key though when choosing a lender and agent.

WHEN A HOME DOES NOT SELL

It may be hard to believe, but some homes just don't sell. In my daily endeavors as a REALTOR® I come across the most beautiful properties. I also come across some questionable homes as well, but we won't get into those homes in this book.

There are some homes that despite all efforts to sell the home, it just doesn't sell. No matter how much it is cleaned, staged, shown, price adjusted, etc., not all homes will sell. What would cause this to happen if the home was beautifully presented for potential buyers? There are some factors that could contribute to a home not selling.

We are going to exclude all the obvious reasons a home doesn't sell, like ugliness, dirty areas and various other eyesores that may be evident. Some of the factors that could cause a beautiful home to NOT sell are timing, price, days on market, not a desirable area, neighbors, and last but certainly not least, availability.

No matter how beautiful a home is, if a buyer is seeing your home, or even driving by and has any bad feeling about the street, area, or neighbors, that could cause them to keep driving by. A house that has been on the market for a long time in an area where it should have gotten a buyer sooner could cause someone to not view the home. If the same type of home is in an area that does not have a large group of buyers, such as a home in the country, then that could be a reason why a beautiful home doesn't sell. Typically, homes in the country tend to take a little longer to sell, because that type of property appeals to a smaller group of buyers.

It is very important for everyone to be honest with each other about the home, the area, and the price. A professional REALTOR® could advise you whether or not it makes sense to sell your home at the price you want. There could be nothing worse than to list your home and go through all the work to sell it, only to find out that the price was too high, the area not in demand, or maybe the house needs a little more work before selling. These are all things that must be considered before deciding to put your home up for sale. You will end up wasting your time if you don't consider all these factors.

SOMETIMES YOU HAVE TO LET A CLIENT GO

I understand that the title of this chapter may have had you doing a double take! Make no mistake, sometimes it is better to part ways if the end goal is not in sight. This works both ways as well should a REALTOR® not put forth their best effort for the client.

One of my first listings that was over $300k provided me with a learning lesson that I will never forget. While a lot of agents are overly eager in obtaining a listing, it was this particular one that taught me that not every seller is motivated to sell.

I had approached a couple that had been selling By Owner with no luck. We got together and I presented them area statistics and information as to what sold, what was on the market, etc. After our initial conversation, they decided to list the home with me. I went over the things I would do to market their home and even offered pointers in prepping the home for better results. Armed with all that knowledge, the sellers, however, failed to do these things. As we progressed through the process of showing their home, just about every potential buyer had the same concerns. After many negative feedback comments shared by buyers' agents, I advised a change to address these concerns; after all, these things were affecting them from getting an offer! This particular couple chose not to take my professional advice and wanted to keep moving forward. The decision to not make these changes made me realize that there was not much chance that this house would sell for the price they wanted, due to the 'concerns' potential buyers were having. With three weeks left in our listing agreement, I withdrew the listing. I notified them that I was doing so and I cut my losses.

As a professional, you have to be willing to walk away from business that will not provide you the result that you need for both parties. I can provide the expertise and tips necessary for a home sale, but if a seller is not willing to do what it takes to sell their home, then both parties lose.

I like to think that I provide solutions for people that have a problem. It has to make sense for the REALTOR® and Seller and/or Buyer to have a solid partnership. Selling a home is a process that requires a little work from the seller and a lot of work from the REALTOR®.

It is in the best interests of both parties that certain expectations are set up front to get the end result that the client and REALTOR® is looking for. Without this way of thinking, it may be just another listing that will sit on the market for a while.

DETERMINING A BUYERS OR SELLERS MARKET

One of the most common questions I get as a real estate professional is "How is the market doing?" or, "Is it a buyer's market, or a seller's market?" Homeowners are always interested in what the market is doing and how it affects them. Even if a homeowner may not be moving in the near future, they still want to know if something is happening in the market. Why do you ask? Because, if something is happening in the market that motivates a homeowner to move sooner, or stay longer, they will want to know that without the surprise.

People often ask me what determines if it is a seller's market, or a buyer's market. There are many factors that go into this. The real estate market has often a see-saw effect where one side benefits over the other. A sellers market simply means that there are more advantages to the seller than there are for the buyer. One of the factors contributing to this is the fact that there are not a lot of homes on the market. This causes buyers to 'fight', or be more aggressive with their offers to purchase a home. This means the seller makes out well.

A buyers market would mean that housing inventory is higher with sellers competing to get buyers in the door. This causes more advantages for the buyer to purchase and, therefore, better deals are had for the home buyer. Several other factors play into this, such as mortgage rates and tax incentives that the government may put in place to spur up some activity in real estate, i.e., the home buyer bonuses that were offered just after the last recession.

A LAZY AGENT CAN COST YOU THOUSANDS OF DOLLARS

I create a weekly value added real estate web show called The AskJasonGelios Real Estate Show. I take questions or topics from clients and viewers and I answer them in video format. One of the shows I had recorded with a local mortgage expert highlighting MSHDA's down payment assistance program got several people to contact me regarding how they can get the program to work for them.

If you are not familiar with what MSHDA is, it is the Michigan State Housing Development Authority. MSHDA is a program that offers a down payment assistance program for home buyers that qualify. It is a program that every home buyer should look into and try to get before they purchase a home.

I remember one particular person who contacted me stated that her son had to close on a home with another agent prior to meeting me and missed out on this available down payment assistance. In this particular situation, I learned that the other agent was not knowledgeable enough to offer that down payment assistance, which means their client missed out on a possible $15,000 towards their down payment!

How did this agent not know about that program? Well it boils down to that particular agent not knowing what is going on in the industry, which poorly affected her buyer. Even worse, her buyer missed out on that good amount of money towards their house.

Often times I see professionals not keeping up to date with what the market is doing or what programs are available to home buyers. It is our duty as real estate professionals to know what is out there for our clients. While I was not able to help this particular person, because they had already closed on a home, it was a reminder of how important it is to stay up to date on my market updates and programs available for home buyers.

YEARS OF EXPERIENCE DON'T ALWAYS ADD UP

I have heard countless people in real estate claim they know a lot, due to their years of experience. Now I doubt real estate is the only industry where this happens, but the truth is, it doesn't matter how many years of experience someone has, because the amount of time someone spends doing something doesn't really make them an expert. Now I know some of you reading this may have a different opinion, and that's ok, but I will continue to share my experiences with other professionals that believe years means experience.

I've seen people in my industry that have used this line often to basically cover a mistake they made, or to hide the fact that they overlooked something that came back to cause an issue for everyone involved. These same professionals hide behind their years of experience to attempt to make themselves look good. Well, while doing this they actually make themselves look worse to those that know they messed up. It doesn't make sense to me to lie or try to use your years of experience to make yourself look better. In real estate, I tend to see this more when a real estate agent sitting down with a potential home seller, points out they have "decades" of experience. Unfortunately, some homeowners actually like that! Wouldn't it make more sense for the agent to actually explain how they will market and cause a buyer to purchase your home? Wouldn't it be better if they went over their marketing plan with the homeowner and provided the benefits the home seller will have vs. sharing that they simply have years of experience? I have come across many people who have years of experience and are absolutely horrible at what they do. Having years of experience really means very little in many cases. Someone could boast decades of experience, but with a poor track record. I'm sure you could name someone you know that falls into this category.

Let me share with you an example of what I mean. In my first year of real estate I sold more than the average agent. The average agent closes about 3-5 deals a year, so if they have multiple years of experience selling on the bottom average, why brag about that? Now there are some agents that have sold a lot and grow their business year after year. And I do know many REALTORS® that do have years of experience and truly know what they are doing. Those are the agents that do the things that provide benefit and value to a potential home buyer or seller. But they sell more than just their years of experience. The ones that only claim to have years of experience are the ones you should run from.

CHEESY MARKETING ONLY GOES SO FAR

If you take a look around, you don't have to look far to see some pretty bold claims from some agents stating they can sell a home faster and for more money than anyone else? While I find this quite amusing that someone can make this claim without even seeing your home, I feel we should talk about this further.

One of the most common things I have seen in cheesy marketing is where an agent states the following "I can sell your home in 30 days or less!" Again, this goes back to how a real estate professional can make this claim without viewing the home. Not all professionals can sell all things. Making this claim suggests that you can sell anything at anytime and that is just not the case. Sure this type of marketing may get the phone to ring a little, but what happens after the agent meets with the homeowner and disappoints them. I have found that most agents who make this bold claim are shooting in the dark hoping the homeowner will call them and choose them to sell their home. They will get you to call and then tell you to put your house on the market for a lot less than what the market would want to pay for it, thus a fast sale. This is not rocket science, yet some agents still do this to get business. I have seen agents in my area implement this technique to get business, instead of taking the more professional approach and consulting to see if they can do the best for the homeowner/potential client. They push ads like this in hopes that the phone will ring.

When looking to sell your home, make sure you have someone that is being honest with you up front and basing their advice on facts, such as numbers in your area. Anybody can put a home on the market for rock bottom to get a quick sale. Always choose the agent that is honest with you about pricing and marketing. Always avoid the type of person that tells you exactly what you want to hear to get you to sign with them. When I meet with someone about selling a home, I provide honesty while backing it up with facts about the area. No fluff or cheesy marketing. This benefits not only the home seller, but also the professional, because no time was really wasted – Win, Win.

BIG NAME OFFICES DON'T ALWAYS MEAN BETTER SERVICE

Some people choose who they will have sell their home by what office they work for. While this makes some sense, due to all the advertising the big name offices do, I am here to tell you that big name offices, or brands, don't always provide better service. I know many big name offices hire a lot of newer agents that have little to no experience, but are happy to have some spots filled in the office.

Big name offices will tell you that they get more exposure on the Internet for your property, or that they have access to more buyers. I am here to tell you that this is a myth. Choosing a real estate professional strictly by the office they represent can be hazardous to your home sale. You always want to base this big decision on whether or not you like the person and what marketing plan they have for your home. Most big name offices provide only training to their agents that most other serious agents get on their own anyway with a smaller office.

You will not get more exposure for your home if the agent does not work to get more buyers looking at it. There is no magic pill big name offices have that small offices don't have. So don't fall for this type of marketing where the big name office touts how many more buyers will see your home. It boils down to the professional you decide to choose. A real estate agent from a big name office can cost a home seller thousands if they don't know what they are doing.

HELP PEOPLE GET WHAT THEY WANT

This section is more of a tip for new or existing professionals. I am a firm believer that if you help enough people get what they want, then it will come back to you ten-fold. This is not to say you should always give to get and expect something in return. It simply means that every day you should give something of value, whether it be something like this book you're reading, or helpful articles on a blog or website. One of the biggest mistakes I see real estate agents and other businesses around me do is ask, ask, ask. They use old school marketing expecting people to contact them. Real estate agents send out generic postcards stating what they sold in the area. While this may be a necessary evil, it should only be a small part of what a professional does. Creating value for potential clients will help someone stand out from the other people in their profession.

A professional that puts out value added content will not only gain more attention from potential clients, they will also build up a personal brand that will last longer than a standard piece of marketing ever will. Value added content is what people want. Not to mention people are very busy these days and they don't want spam content that brags only about the sender.

A GOOD REALTOR®
COMMUNICATES EFFECTIVELY

One of my clients closed on a beautiful ranch home that fit their needs perfectly. The former owner who sold the home with the assistance of her agent had agreed to a 10-day occupancy. This meant the owner, who signed off on the home at closing, had to surrender the keys to the home no more than ten days post closing. While this is what the agent had stated there seemed to be some delay as we approached the deadline.

The seller stated that they needed more time to get their items out and move into their next home. This worried my buyer client, because they were anticipating moving in and had made arrangements to do so. The former owner provided many reasons why they should not have agreed to the ten-day occupancy when the home was placed under contract with their agent. After much conversing back and forth, we were able to offer a few extra days and the seller moved out at that time. One of the takeaways from this situation is to always make sure every detail is communicated accurately before the process begins. In this case, the former owner could have communicated better with their agent that they would need more time after closing to move out.

Many agents miss parts of the process because they often get so happy to list a home on the market, that they tend to rush the client through the initial signing. They may or may not be doing this on purpose, but it should not be something that occurs. Confidence is key and if you choose to work with someone that is held to a higher standard, they should make every effort to ensure that the client knows exactly what is going on throughout all the steps of this process.

In this case with the short term deadline to move out, had this person been represented properly, this issue of having to move out faster than they thought probably would not have come up. These are just some of the situations that need to be taken into consideration BEFORE a seller's home hits the market.

CASH IS NOT ALWAYS KING

You may have heard on cable TV shows, or in your everyday conversations, that when purchasing a home Cash Is King. Shows like 'Million Dollar Listing' show the agents often bragging about a cash offer and a quick close.

While cash offers do provide less headaches and faster closes, they often do not benefit the seller. Cash offers come with a much lower offer on price, compared to a financed offer. In my own real estate career, I have seen cash deals come in tens of thousands of dollars less with the investor, or buyer, holding strong because it is a cash offer.

Some sellers may be seduced at a chance to take a loss just to close on the deal faster. However, most home sellers prefer a higher offer that nets them more money after closing, even if it means they have to wait a little longer for the process.

In some selling situations I've been in I have been able to bring an investor up higher and closer to the asking price, but this is rare. This was also in a seller's market as the inventory was low. When considering a cash offer, make sure it benefits you and your situation. The last thing you want is regret that you jumped on a much lower offer when other offers may have come in and netted you more money.

A DEAL WHERE CASH WAS NOT KING

I had a cute small house that I had listed in a little community that was gaining a lot of attraction. The showings were almost back to back on many of the days over the course of two weeks. We were at a pretty good market price and the home had a ton of potential. One particular day I received a call from a buyer's agent stating his client was interested in placing an offer. I welcomed the conversation and recommended they present an offer same day, as we were about to have multiple offers on the home. After some hours had passed, the buyer's agent sent over a poorly put together purchase agreement/offer with a note in the email stating that his client was an all cash buyer wanting the home at a considerably less price than what we were willing to accept. After receiving this offer, and other offers I might add, my seller decided to move on to another offer that was more favorable. As I relayed this news to the buyer's agent, that is when all hell broke loose. The buyer's agent began rattling on about how a cash buyer is king and we should just accept his client's offer. After hearing this from the agent, I simply stated some of the reasons why my seller did not choose to accept his client's offer. This particular agent got in his own way, and that of the client, by not being properly prepared. They sent over an offer without proof of funds, something all cash buyers should have, and without the sellers' disclosures signed.

Furthermore, the offer price was a lot less than what my seller was willing to accept. After hours of reviewing multiple offers, my client moved forward on a lender financed deal that favored the seller and the buyer. This is just one example of how cash is not always king. Oftentimes cash buyers offer a lot less than what a property is on the market for, in hopes to make their money up front. After all, that is when real estate investors make the most money on the deal.

SUCCESS DOES NOT REWARD LAZINESS

A friend of mine had referred me to a potential home seller who was thinking of hiring another REALTOR® that she had dealt with on the purchase of her current home years prior. She had some reservation about moving forward with the other agent and contacted me to sit down with her. She thought it would be a good idea to meet with me, because I came as a no obligation referral and my insight may help her in her decision. I remember meeting with her at her home one winter evening to discuss what she was looking to do in detail. We were talking about the potential for me to sell her home and some of the marketing I would do for the home. I remember her telling me that she had worked with an agent before who she was unsure about working with again. When I had asked her why she had reservations, she stated some of the things that bothered her. She had reached out to this agent prior to being referred to me. She expressed interest in selling her home and purchasing a home that would be closer to her kids' school. She had hoped that this agent would have wanted to schedule a time to sit down and talk about the process and what to expect. This was this homeowners' first time selling a home.

While she had expected this process to take place with the other agent, it simply did not. She had received a text back from that agent with a suggested selling price and a comment stating that when she was ready to list the home, he would get the documents over to her via email. This certainly did not impress this homeowner.

This was just one of the things that made her unsure about

whether the other agent was the professional she wanted to sell her home. What happened here was that the other agent expressed laziness through his bad approach of the process of selling her home. Even worse, was his disregard for the fact that this was her first time selling a home and that she was looking for more than just a vague and lazy recommendation. He had blown any chance of selling her home at this point.

She may have once had a good experience with him when he helped her locate her current home, but he did absolutely nothing to keep providing value after the deal was closed. He had become lazy. He was assuming she would just have him list the home and failed to assess the situation, or offer more of what she wanted.

This agent made no effort to come out and meet with her or even pull up some area numbers to show her what was on the market in her area. This made her uncomfortable and even question his professionalism, because it seemed as though he didn't want to do the work necessary to sell her home.

Selling a home is a big deal and one of the things that professionals should do is sit down with the homeowner and actually walk them through the process. This agent neglected to see that this was her first time selling a home and, therefore, just assumed she would put the house on the market with him, because he helped her out several years before.

As we were talking about some of the methods that I would use to sell her home, she decided that I was the perfect representative for her. As I got everything in place to put the house on the market, we had already gained attraction to it. This action resulted in a multiple offer situation within seven days! While every house sale may not work this way, a home seller deserves every effort a true professional can provide to sell the home fast. There is no excuse to work with someone who will do the minimum, or less. I remember my client telling me that when the house hit the market, the other agent texted her and asked her why she decided to go with another agent. While she never really responded back to him, I could tell you that it was because success does not reward laziness. When an agent does not go above and beyond or becomes complacent, they just won't get the business, or shouldn't get the business.

Every real estate transaction that I have been involved with has been a big deal whether it was a $400,000 home, or a $60,000 home. Buying and selling real estate are big transactions to everyone involved and one of the biggest financial processes that a person may experience.

When a homeowner or prospective homeowner wishes to work with an agent, an agent should do everything that they can to help make the client comfortable.

MORTGAGE EXPERIENCE MATTERS

Prior to my real estate career, I had the privilege of working many years in the mortgage industry. I met a lot of great professionals and still remain in contact with them. I had the opportunity to learn the business inside and out, both on the wholesale and retail side. I also had the opportunity to meet a great number of people who were purchasing homes and/or consolidating debt with lower interest rates and better options.

All the in-depth training and experience I gained through that time has been crucial to offering the best advice for my clients. Even to this day I keep up on the latest mortgage offerings and programs. Not to mention the ever changing regulations! Many REALTORS® that I know keep up on the latest mortgage information, because it benefits who we work with. Knowing the differences between various mortgage options and the short and long term affects are what benefits a client.

My buyers can feel more secure knowing that I have the experience in lending, which makes for a much more comfortable situation when shopping for a home. While many things have changed in terms of regulations and guidelines, the basics of lending and what mortgage options are available and what they can do, has remained almost the same.

Not everyone fits into the same mortgage. With so many options available it can also be overwhelming to a home buyer, which can lead to confusion. One has to actually know the benefit of what each loan can provide the client. Good REALTORS® will be able to either explain the basics of these programs, or refer their client to a reputable mortgage expert who will work in their best interests.

While not all REALTORS® will have the background in mortgages, a home buyer will want to make sure they either work with a lender that is knowledgeable and a REALTOR® who knows the basics of lending and some common requirements. One example of this would be FHA loans requiring an FHA licensed appraiser to conduct the appraisal. This type of appraiser will check to make sure the home is FHA approved.

Some of the right questions to ask your REALTOR® and mortgage expert are "Are there any down payment assistance programs available? Have you had experience assisting home buyers with down payment assistance programs? Which mortgage is best for my situation?" When a home buyer asks these questions it better prepares them for the home buying process.

I recall one particular situation where my experience with the mortgage side benefitted one of my clients. A couple looking to purchase their first home were thrilled at the possibility to go with a VA mortgage loan. VA is a great option for veterans who are not looking to put a large amount of money down on the home. After getting our offer accepted on the home they chose and moving along in the process, I started noticing some discrepancies with the lender and what they were asking my client to do for the mortgage. I had mentioned to my clients that some things were not adding up and then things got worse. The lender had advised my clients they might not be able to get the home, because of some credit matters. By this point my clients were stunned and very upset. How could this have happened so far into the transaction? How did they get preapproved at the beginning only to be told they may not be able to purchase this home? After speaking with my clients, they agreed to get a second opinion. They reached out to a lender that I happened to know and started the process all over again with them. After the lender looked at my clients' situation and pulled credit, it was realized that they fit into another program, This meant they would be able to get the deal done and closing on the home. After hearing this news, my clients were thrilled! It was at this point that my clients let the other lender know they were making the switch. The deal closed and they were relieved that everything worked out fine.

SOME FINAL THOUGHTS

I hope you enjoyed reading this book as much as I enjoyed writing it. My main focus of this book was to provide you with the information you need to make more educated decisions when you are looking to buy, or sell, real estate. Too often people choose the wrong professional, or receive the wrong information, which results in a bad experience.

If you are a real estate professional new to the business, or have been doing this for awhile, I hope this book aids you in raising the bar in your own career. People want value and they want to see what you can do for them. There is always room to grow in the real estate industry and we should never be complacent.

While it seems like real estate agents are a dime a dozen, there are really only a small amount that show up to work and work really hard and smart. Many agents come and go in the real estate industry. Buyers and sellers often get hurt when matched up with the wrong agent. Due diligence is key when choosing someone to help you buy, or sell, a home. When it comes to one of the biggest transactions you will be involved in, don't leave this to chance. Real estate is not just about knowing the numbers; it's about building relationships. The most important thing that I strive for is finding out what a client/potential client's goal is when buying or selling a home. If you are looking to purchase or sell a home, work with someone who is not only experienced, but also one that markets in the year we live in. Peoples focus and attention change all the time. With the rise of social media and Internet driven activity, you want someone who stays on top of these marketing trends to get the most exposure for your home. At the end of the day, a home sale is caused by getting the attention which creates the buyer demand. Of course the home has to look nice too.

This is more than a quick read.

This book is not just a one time read and throw it on your shelf. It is a book to be studied. It is a book to be shared. It is a resource for you so that you can make a more educated decision when you are buying or selling real estate or choosing the right professional. This book was written for you so that you can benefit from the information provided.

Thank you again for reading my book! Please feel free to reach out to me should you have questions or comments.

I wish you the best of luck in your real estate endeavors!

JASON GELIOS

REALTOR®

Jason Gelios is a top producing Michigan REALTOR® serving Detroit, Michigan and surrounding areas. Jason works with home buyers and sellers to help accomplish their goals of buying or selling real estate. He also works with people looking to rent homes short and long term.

ON THE INTERNET

Jason's website www.ItsAllAboutTheRealEstate.com is a wealth of information and also the best way to reach out to Jason. You can also find the latest videos uploaded here.

ON SOCIAL MEDIA

Jason shares valuable information regarding real estate tips and home maintenance tips on his social media outlets.

YouTube: Search 'Jason Gelios'
Facebook: https://www.facebook.com/jasongeliosrealtor/
Twitter: https://twitter.com/jasongelios
Instagram: https://www.instagram.com/jasongelios/
Pinterest: https://www.pinterest.com/jasongelios/
LinkedIn: https://www.linkedin.com/in/jasongelios

PUBLIC SPEAKER

Jason speaks at local home buyer events such as the MSU (Michigan State University) extension offering home buying tips to participants.

MONTHLY E-NEWSLETTER

Jason produces a free monthly e-newsletter that shares tips from home maintenance to real estate knowledge. Visit www.ItsAllAboutTheRealEstate.com to subscribe.

THE ASKJASONGELIOS REAL ESTATE SHOW

Jason produces a weekly internet show offering advice and answering questions for his viewers. You can follow and subscribe by visiting www.ItsAllAboutTheRealEstate.com and on social media.

TOP PRODUCER ACKNOWLEDGMENT

Jason has been recognized by his local MLS and office as a top producing professional.

RESOURCES

ItsAllAboutTheRealEstate.com
Value packed advice, tips and videos and the best way to reach out to Jason for real estate inquiries. Also the main hub for the AskJasonGelios Real Estate Show

AskJasonGelios Real Estate Show
Weekly episodes uploaded to the major social media networks. Sometimes special guests drop by to share valuable advice too!

MSHDA (Down Payment Assistance in Michigan)
For down payment assistance in the State Of Michigan please visit https://www.michigan.gov/mshda/.

Foreclosure help and information
If you are in need of mortgage payment assistance please visit https://www.fdic.gov/consumers/assistance/protection/mortgages/fc-prevention/consumer.html.

Credit report information
By federal law you are allowed one free copy of your credit report from each agency every 12 months. The only authorized website to obtain that without a charge is AnnualCreditReport.com.

WHAT PEOPLE ARE SAYING ABOUT JASON

Jason is very knowledgeable about the real estate business. He was very professional and worked hard to spotlight our home in the best light and reach out to the most people in order to make a quick sale. He was always available and we were very pleased with his service. *- Patricia B.*

Jason is very professional from start to finish. He gave us excellent advise and we had a offer on our house in less than 12 hours! He also helped us find our dream home. He goes above and beyond. I highly recommend him! *- Brian & Shawn*

Jason continuously went above and beyond with the sale of our home. The experience was seamless and he backed all of his recommendations with real life examples for us to see. We have had so-so experiences with home sales/purchasing in the past- and we thought those dealings were great or standard until we worked with Jason. His dedication and availability were far above par and the overall experience was much better for us. We have recommended him to others looking to buy or sell and will use him in the future for any realty needs. *- Stephen and Sarah N.*

Thank you, Thank you!

There are multiple people to whom I would like to say Thank you, Thank you!

To my wife Erica

You always inspire me to be a better version of my last self and for being my better half. Without you I would not be half the person that I am today. We sure have come a long way. I love you!

To my wonderful children Haley and Jayden

You both inspire me daily when I see you learning new things and accomplishing your own goals. You both are going to be a great success. Remain focused and pursue your dreams!

To my parents James and Karen

You always believed that I would turn out to be something good and you always taught me the value of hard work and the importance of family. You are the best parents a son could have. I love you both!

Michael and Patricia Gordon

You are always available for me to bounce ideas off of and for always having an open ear. Also a huge thank you to you Patricia Gordon for proofreading and editing this book. Your suggestions took my rough draft and made it a better version of itself.

To my sister Sharon Robinson

You always encourage me to do great things. You are the best sister a brother could have. Stay true to yourself and keep hitting your goals you set. Love you sis!

To all my friends and family

I have been truly blessed with great friends and family that stand by me. I enjoy our time together and I look forward to what the future brings for our relationships.

My family of clients

It has been a pleasure helping you buy and/or sell real estate. I look forward to continuing to be your honest and reliable resource when you need real estate questions answered or a professional on your side.

My colleagues

The real estate industry is a lot easier when you have the right professionals and resources at your disposal. I appreciate all of you that have played a part in helping me grow my business.

Thank you, Thank You!

"Our job as real estate professionals is to provide a much higher level of service and professionalism to our clients which is owed."

JASON GELIOS